The Light at the end of the bowl

Written by Bert Fish

Illustrated by C Giffin

The Choir Press

Copyright © 2025 Bert Fish

All rights reserved. No part of this publication may be reproduced or transmitted in any form or by any means, electronic or mechanical including photocopying, recording or any information storage or retrieval system, without prior permission in writing from the publishers.

The right of Bert Fish to be identified as the author of this work has been asserted by him in accordance with the Copyright, Designs and Patents Act 1988

First published in the United Kingdom in 2025 by
The Choir Press

ISBN 978-1-78963-583-6

Preface

The story I am about to tell you is a true story.
At times it appears to be the stuff of fiction but alas I can't lie.
I believe everyone has a story and this is mine.
So where did it begin? To tell you this I have to go back to the beginning. I was born in 1970 in Redhill, Surrey in June.
Nothing spectacular you may think? I was ordinary, living in an ordinary house with 3 older siblings, Mum and Dad. Out of respect for my late mother, I have written about my childhood in the book so I am not going to talk about that for now. All seemed well, I had 2 parents, older siblings, we even had 2 dogs. Dad was a lecturer at a college and Mum took care of us. There were problems though, some of which I witnessed at a very early age. You see all was not well with the family.
Dad would disappear and I never knew why. I can still remember Dad coming home from work and giving me a lift on his motorcycle. I was always happy to see him but this didn't last. Let us fast forward to when I was around 2/3 years old. Dad and Mum were talking, however I sensed something was wrong. Dad had a bag with him and they where talking at the front door. Dad asked Mum "is this what you want", and Mum said "yes". Even being so young I could sense there was a problem, Dad was going and he walked out of the door, carrying his bag. I went into the front room and stared out of the window. Dad was sitting in his car, engine running but not moving. I assumed he was getting something from the car.
After what seemed like an age he started to drive off.
I ran to the front door, and with a mighty effort I opened the door. I ran up the road screaming "Daddy don't go".
I can still remember it like it was yesterday and I still feel it.
This was my first feeling of abandonment and it followed me everywhere ever since.

Mum and Dad had split up, I was devastated. This was the start of a very long and lonely journey. I started self harming and really playing up.

We where raised on welfare and Mum worked 3 jobs just to provide for us.

Welfare in the 70's was very tough but I got through school somehow despite the constant bullying. I wasn't very academic but the one thing I was good at was sports, mainly football. I played for all my school football teams and when I left school I played for my local team. I wasn't good with relationships and would have a string of girlfriends, although these never lasted long. I had abandonment issues and low self esteem and it was at this point I started to drink heavily, but also attempt suicide frequently. I cannot say whether I was born an alcoholic but I like to think I just wanted to fit in. I started getting in trouble with the law, ending in 2 prison sentences. I met a wonderful woman at this point and we started a family even though I was about to do time. I couldn't take the pressure and I took a massive overdose. Clinically I was dead for 4 minutes and my kidneys failed. My partner was devastated and it nearly cost the relationship. Luckily for me she waited for me and visited me in prison every 2 weeks, also writing every day. She is the strongest woman I have ever met and when I came home we moved, having another daughter and I got a good job. There was a glaring problem though, my mental health. Due to my drinking I was not diagnosed correctly, just seen as a trouble maker. I got into gambling, self harming and drinking. I am pleased to say I no longer gamble or drink. I still self harm but that is between me and my Dr. I have a diagnoses and I take medication for this and currently have a nice place to live, which is a miracle. My daughters are grown up now and in a way so am I. I wish I could say there is a happy ending but alas I split with their mother. So here I am, my story, my life and no lies.

I hope you enjoy reading about my journey.

Afraid to feel

When the train left the station I missed it
When the boat left the shore I weren't there
When the bus came along I was having my fun
So for now I don't really care.

When the party was on I weren't going
Cause I had somewhere else I could be
Always had a voice but still making no choice
I go through life flippant, care free.

The plane will fly out in the morning
But again I will give it a miss
Not leaving today, cause I'm running away
Once again I have broken my promise.

Can't seem to face up to my demons
Running scared is the easiest way
We could set a date but you know I'll be late
All I do now is live for today.

When you wanted to go to a nightclub
I'd go to our local instead
One day I just may, think of something to say
And explain what goes on in my head.

Afraid to feel

On my arm is the prettiest woman
But love don't come easy to me
Self-destructive today, I sent you away,
I can't see the wood for the trees.

I told you I'd do it tomorrow
That tomorrow has passed by a year
For once if I'd only, stop being so lonely
And face up and tackle my fears.

If I stumble along will you be there
Will you help me if I make that call?
Not sure what to do so I'm counting on you
I'm scared if I let go I'll fall.

Another train waits at the station
This one it waits specially for me
In the harbour there's moored a boat I can board
That will take me where I need to be.

The crossroads of life I've arrived at
You've shown me the path I must take
But still I conceal, the pain that I feel
The decision that I need to make.

Is whether I choose to remain here?
Or trust in the way I've been shown
Hold onto my hand, but please understand
Run away is all I have known

But that train is now leaving the station
And the boat is sailing away too
But do not despair, for I've paid my fare
Now this time I'll be travelling with you.

Holiday

The last time that
I went abroad Was 1991
Off to the Canary Islands
With mates to get some sun.

I've never been abroad before
Only holidays I had
Was caravan or camping trips
With either mum or dad.

Departed for the airport lounge
To catch our early flight
Excited at the prospect of
Flying late at night.

Before we leave some duty free
Southern Comfort, cigarettes
I've dipped into my budget
I hope I don't regret it.

My case packed full of goodies as
I don't trust the local food
A shot of Whiskey on the flight
To get me in the mood.

The flight is only 4 hours long
I've managed several drinks
Is this the start of heavy stuff
Reach apartment for more drinks.

Wake up all bleary eyed
The welcome has begun
We sign up to some excursions
They sound like lots of fun.

Holiday

We booked up lots of trips that day
With lots of things to do
From beach party, to meal to cruise
There's plenty to keep us amused.

We settle down to our routine
It starts with bacon rolls
Then lounge around the pool all day
Cocktails, shower then shows.

One trip I'm looking forward too
Is go karting with the boss
I think I'm something special
Like a younger Stirling Moss.

We have a safe for passports
And 6 bottles of harder drink
In case we run out of supplies
In the fridge under the sink.

Every night we all roll back
At maybe 4 or 5
2 Weeks of massive benders
Not sure I will survive.

We lounge around the pool at 10
To top up on our tan
Get ready for the night to come
We never have a plan.

Holiday

The date is looming fast for me
My 21st birthday night
6 Nightclubs synchronize clocks for me
It really was a sight.

The days we spend just lounging round
With cocktails in our hands
I could get quite used to this
A drink, top up our tans.

We hired a 4x4 one day
To go to Santa Cruz
To spend the day at water park
We were stopped for breaking rules.

We started every evening
Eating loads of vodka jelly
Washed down with Southern Comfort
One more and then we are ready.

The night life only minutes
From apartments where we stay
Palm tree shortcut to the beach
The highlight of the day.

We've settled in quite nicely
The routine that we do
The 2nd week more arrivals
Was the time that I met you.

Holiday

Your name unknown from Derby
I think your very cute
We kissed and danced together
No need to wear my suite.

We spent a week together
Stayed by each other's side
For you its holiday romance
For me it's hard to hide.

Not saying that I used you
I think I cared as much
I still have all the photos that
You sent to stay in touch.

The thing that I found really tough
When I was going home
No job, income or future
I have nothing but a loan

The time was passing quickly now
My time of sunny haze
The flight home looming fast for me
Goodbye to sunny days.

When I was there I borrowed
More money for my jaunt
Going home I had nothing
Not worried it's not my fault.

Holiday

I drank so much when I was there
I had a lovely time
The memories and the photographs
The holiday yours and mine.

One sunny summer hot day
Linnekers was the name
Geoff and I wore Palace tops
To go and watch the game.

But didn't know that Barca
Was being shown instead
A bar of 8 supporters
Were watching, god we're dead.

We'd met so many people
We'll meet up in your flat
Nothing but a tan for me
And a statement on the mat.

I loved the 2 weeks whilst away
I blocked out the truest fact
My drinking got quite unbearable
And I cannot pay you back.

Charlotte

October 12th the day in question
A date when understand the lesson
Emotions running very high
A love like this lights up the sky.

My precious girl, so perfect and calm
Cradled in your mother's arms
I've never felt so proud before
You need my love, I'll give you more.

My life complete cause now I'm daddy,
Embrace accept this challenge gladly
Shower you with all our love
Angelic girl, sent from up above.

If ever I get down and blue
Just close my eyes and think of you
I'll always be there by your side
So happy bursting with such pride.

Looking forward to being a dad
I know sometimes you may get sad
That if you fall and start to cry
We'll do our best and always try.

As I sit here I feel so grand
Gently clasp your tiny hand
We'll dress you up in pretty frocks
With bow in hair and matching socks.

Charlotte

A lucky man I am tonight
To gaze upon your wondrous sight
You've won my heart like no-one could
Protect and love as fathers should.

I don't know what the future holds
To be a dad but no one told
Just how much of my heart you'd take
I'll do my best make no mistake.

Arriving home the news has broke
No longer am I just a bloke
Simon first then Angela too
An aunty once again for you.

There will be highs and maybe lows
But we'll love you, buy the greatest clothes
Cindy sits on guard duty
Two left home but now there's three.

One by one the visits begin.
First your nan then friends come in
Poor Cindy has her work to do
Without a fuss you won't come through.

I never will forget this night
We'll always make sure you're alright
Achieved a lot as boy and man
But this is the day my life began.

Homeless

There is a man lives in our town
You'll never see him wear a frown
A coffee cup, a bench to sit
He'll drink his cup and ponder it.

At this point doing just fine
No need to carry on with time
Stop right here and have my drink
Don't mind if I just sit and think.

The coffee sweet I feel quite humble
Not one to moan won't hear me grumble
Thank you for this one small thing
Right now sat here feel like a king.

Won't eat tonight but that is then
Until that time we're equal men
Maybe soon I'll get that break
A place called home a bed to make.

This life for me is very real
Just need some clothes and a hot meal
And maybe if I got my chance
Get things moving and make a stance.

But watch you stare as you go past
You wonder will I be the last
Don't want your type around this place
I see it written on your face.

Homeless

There is no other place to go
Maybe one day you never know
Just half a chance that's all I need
You'll see I'm not consumed with greed.

Easy in life to lose the lot
Become the man you all forgot
Shuffle along the lonely road
A life reaped from the past I sowed.

If you were me and I was you
Then would you know just what to do
To take me from this lonely life
And find me somewhere warm and nice.

Without a home I'm nothing more
Then pigeons that scavenge from the floor
For with each day that I stay here
Day's to months and months to years.

I have my seat there's space for you
If you join me and listen too
The man you see before you there
Had a life and used to care.

Just need to feel some part and love
I always pray to him above
Look after me my soul to keep
And one day get me off this street.

Tomorrow

Your actions for the day just gone
Could help change someone's future
Good or bad or feeling sad
A person's life you can nurture.

Today consigned to our history
When the sun set's on the day
Before setting sun look back what you've done
Did you help your friends all of the way.

Tomorrow the future's not written
Will you help the world with a good deed?
Try not to feel blue, regret nothing new
As nothing in life's guaranteed.

If it seems to go wrong just forget it
For it can't go right all of the time
Do the best that you can, and lend helping hands
If you help then tomorrow you'll shine.

Tomorrow is just in the distance
The history can be written by you
Don't let slip away, regret didn't say
For yesterday has gone away too.

The history books we can learn from
It's easy to look back with sorrow
The history we're making, it's yours for the taking
So what will you do come tomorrow.

Tomorrow

Your choices could influence people
Just maybe you'll show the right way
New day starts tomorrow, but which will you follow
Your heart or the mood of the day.

If I told you I'd do it tomorrow
Believe me I'll make it my aim
So goodnight to you, I'll try to be true
And do it for love and not fame.

If you get it wrong don't fret and panic
Don't accept it and blame it on fate
It's nothing un-known, as we are all prone
Most important you learn from mistakes.

There's one thing in life that is certain
The routine, the life that we follow
The way we behave, whether gracious or brave
If you're wrong then there's always tomorrow.

So don't fret and panic it's over
The day has passed by in a flash
You can make a change, it isn't so strange
To regret and rue being so rash

The answer could really be simple
If you worry too much for today
Tomorrow not given, your plan you have written
The cost for tomorrow you'll pay.

Late night call

I do not mind that you called me.
I don't mind you calling at all.
You're life in a rut, but please don't give up.
I thank you for making the call.

I know it's the dead of the night time.
For it doesn't bother one bit.
If you trust in me, I'll go make some tea.
I will listen to you while I sip.

I know on another day pending.
I know that I never had time.
Not a soul will I tell, because your not well.
I'll make sure that your doing just fine.

I know in these early hours calling.
But that doesn't play on my brain.
I'll get out of bed, the kitchen I'll head.
I will listen and try to be sane.

We all have our problems and troubles.
We all have our hopes and our fears.
So just let it out, I won't scream and shout.
Just be patient and wipe away tears.

I'm grateful you feel you can call me.
I'm grateful cause I am your friend.
For I will not share, your hopes or despair.
Whether 2 in the morning or 10.

Late night call

The fact that your calling me so late.
Shows to me just how much you trust.
So do not delay, let it out and just say.
The healing for you is a must.

Not sure that I have all the answers.
But you trust me and so I will try.
If you just want a chat, for you that's a fact.
Don't you worry if you want to cry.

If you need to I'm here I will listen.
If you need to you know I will be here.
Don't mind if you do, as your feeling so blue.
Let it out pal you can bend my ear.

I've never heard you feeling so lonely.
I know that your life is a mess.
But baring your soul, is my only goal.
Is to listen and let out your stress.

Don't panic you needed to call me.
Share your burden and your misery.
It's never too late, for not feeling great.
Just a chat and then maybe you'll see.

You've made it this far on your journey.
So if I can carry you through.
Next stage in your quest, forget all the rest.
Its okay that you feel a bit blue.

Late night call

The loneliest path that your walking.
The journey you take on your own.
So sharing your burden, then all of a sudden.
I am there you are not all alone.

We'll talk until your feeling better.
You have my attention and time.
The time it don't matter, we can talk, we can natter.
We'll continue until you are fine.

If you want to you can call me tomorrow.
You can call me the day or the night.
We can meet for a coffee, no need to feel lonely.
For your burden I'll stand up and fight.

Your not alone that much is certain.
We all have our burden to bare.
If you call for a chat, you know I'll do that.
You know that I'll always be there.

I'm feeling quite useful and humble.
I'm happy that you've chosen me.
We can meet in the morning, your not being boring.
We can do coffee or maybe a tea.

You know you can lean on me brother.
Depend on me that much is true.
Your never alone, in your grasp use your phone.
And call me if your feeling blue.

Late night call

The lesson in life is quite simple.
Make a call to a friend for a chat.
Don't face it alone, the future unknown.
If you do this there's no going back.

The lesson is really straight forward.
A burden is easy to share.
Your life you will manage, despite all the damage.
Don't worry and do not despair.

If your worried about our discussion.
Don't worry I'll keep it with me.
I won't tell a soul, gossips not my goal.
Just confide then a future you'll see.

Can I call you if I have a problem.
As some days I too can be down.
As I need to be, not anxious but free.
When I'm low you can tell from my frown.

Some days other people have issues.
For life has its ups and its lows.
But some days I can't, fix a problem and start.
And get on with all of my woes.

Don't worry my friend if I'm needed.
You know that I'll always be there.
With others I'll take, I'll make no mistake.
As sometimes life just isn't fare.

The M word

People say it's one in four.
In my experience it's probably more.
That's lots of people suffering.
A daily battle some don't win.

It strikes at will creeps up on you.
It's not a normal saddened blue.
Never say "it won't be me."
The futures something we can't see.

It's mental when I ponder back
My monthly trial with doctor Tatch
As far as you're concerned I'm fine
Just wasting pills and precious time.

I know that every now and then
A new shrink will be holding that pen
I'm looking forward to when you're gone
So someone else can get it wrong.

Don't have much faith, why should I care
Another reason for despair
The post is here, appointment through
Don't know this doctor, must be new.

So sitting here the waiting room
A magazine it's my turn soon
Please don't make the same mistake
Or my crisis house awaits.

The M word

You called me mister, shook my hand
Are you the one to understand?
Went through my notes to educate
Worked out the previous mistake.

Could this be the point of change?
The social worker all arranged
I know deep down I can achieve
If someone else would just believe.

You diagnosed me, got it right
So when I go to bed tonight
This is the point it all begins
Dare I dream of happy things?

My personality borderline.
Skate on the edge most of the time.
So take my pills to keep me calm.
And stop me committing my self-harm.

With a social worker on board
No longer will I be ignored
If you will fight then so will I
Cause every avenue I've tried.

I didn't have much hope before
Until you strolled through doctors door
I've never met someone like you
You seem to know just what to do.

The M word

Don't need to fight this thing alone
As you have proved it can be done
When you arrived St Margaret
From now on there's no word called can't.

Your tireless searching, constantly
Trying to sort a home for me
Paid off at last, soon moving in
From this point on I can begin.

The forms are signed, I have my key
A place called home, somewhere for me
And just as soon as you arrived
It's time to say a fond goodbye

So can you guard against insane?
You've more chance guessing sun or rain.
If only someone finds a cure,
For madness we could save loads more.

The miff of illness all too clear.
As people live their lives in fear.
That should they meet someone who's ill.
Is the blame for all societies kill?

But if you knew the truth about me.
And others in society.
More likely to get hit by a bus.
Then come to harm from one of us

My life in comedy

I grew up in the 70's.
We'd all sit around the telly.
Waiting for our favourite show.
After dinner eating jelly.

There's one thing that the Brits do best.
So after my hot bath.
Our sense of family comedy.
Will always make us laugh.

From game shows hosted by the best.
2 Ronnies, Morecombe and Wise.
Dick Emery skates right on the edge.
Always brace for a surprise.

Even adverts can be fun.
Lemonade, ice Campari.
Rossiter and Dame Joan Collins.
On a flight to somewhere sunny.

Tell them about the honey mummy.
It always makes me grin.
I think mum's got the boredom.
As she's opened up the Gin.

My life in comedy

Mum's fave was Richard Digance.
Who'd know that some years later.
I'd take her to the latest scene.
She loves the songs and banter.

Steptoe and son close to the edge.
It's the comedy of the time.
Can't get away with that thing now.
Back then it was just fine.

Only had 3 channels then.
But that was just enough.
To get our fill of comedy night.
The laughter and the mirth.

I always share next day at school.
Did you watch the box last night.
I missed the funny stuff because.
Dad wanted to watch the fight.

We finally got a 4th channel.
To add to the small list.
But nothing funny on that side.
You like but I will miss.

Instead there's spitting image now.
It's a new show full of puns.
Take the Mick out of everyone.
So I tape it, share the fun.

My life in comedy

The 80's are upon us now.
The shows are getting tasty.
The jokes, put downs and sometimes jibes.
They really are quite racy.

I want to see the latest film.
The one they wouldn't pardon.
The church where really mad about.
I think it's called the life of Brian.

A program friends all talk about.
Is the young one's , college students.
Rick, Neil, Mike and Vivian.
They are skint but very prudent.

Not forgetting SPG
The hamster of the punk.
They get in loads of scrapes for sure.
But you never see them drunk.

Not the 9 o'clock news tonight.
I heard about at school.
Their really very funny.
Rowan Atkinson playing the fool.

Alas that show comes to an end.
Don't think I could be sadder.
But the genius that is Rowan.
Comes back as Lord Blackadder.

My life in comedy

It's fair to say, back in the day.
Offensive, racial slightly.
The shows we'd watch no matter what.
I'm viewing telly nightly.

Our family has a humour that.
Skates upon the edge.
My mum prefers the older stuff.
For me it's father Ted.

Jack Dee, Hunter and Jo Brand.
On live at the apollo.
It's live on telly every week.
The program that I follow.

I wondered when my girls where born.
Would their humour be the same.
One likes the film top secret and
The other one air plane.

Blazing saddles, camp fire sketch.
The one about the beans.
The singing horse called Mario.
My daughters like those scenes.

So many years, so long ago.
My brothers came to see.
Jimmy Carr, the Harlequin.
A stand up comedy.

I have a sense of humour still.
It's the only thing I pass.
Not gloomy just a chuckle.
To my girls let's have a laugh.

The greatest song of all time

What is the greatest song of all?
Maybe songs you heard at school
A slushy one or thumping beat
A track to make you stomp your feet.

Perhaps a thought provoking one
That takes you back to golden sun
Or even back to your first kiss
The school disco you never miss.

Could it be a classic song?
With lyrics you can sing along
Or is it one that lifts you up
Get on the dance floor, give a strut.

Could it be from childhood past?
The one you had to give a blast
On the telly, top of the pops
Watching, hoping never stops.

Like the look of that boy band
They sound quite good but dad can't stand
Listen to it on the wireless
Sunday night it's never tireless.

Is it the song that brings out tears?
Relate to even after years
Or the fashion of the time
Don't matter if the words don't rhyme.

The greatest song of all time

What is the song you love the best
The one that stands out from the rest
I don't think anyone will know
It could be one from years ago.

In summer days just lying there
With ice cream and a suntan glare
Turn on your tunes and go way back
And listen to your favourite track

If I feel sad I'll sometimes play
My favourite tune to save the day
A party or your vows divine
You've saved it for a special time.

Share it with your family
And maybe they can feel and see
Just one more track before your bed
Sip your cocoa and rest your head

If you dream about your song
Then you know this is the one
Hold it tight don't let it go
And maybe you just didn't know

What is the greatest ever tune?
Stick around I'll tell you soon
The song you can relate most to
Is the song that's playing just for you.

Roll of the dice

I always love the fun fair
With rides and slot machines,
The weather, rides, don't really care
It's the gambling for my needs.

We'd play the slots and gamble,
I do not really care
I know that I'm not able,
As the odds are just not fair.

The jackpot that I'm aiming for
To get my high and fix
Leave it mate, "no just one more"
The boxes that I tick.

In life I started early, young,
I need my fix and rush
I'll gamble all until I'm done,
Lost it all but not enough.

I do not care if I can't pay,
If I'm not gambling then I'm bored
At the end of another gambling day
The race ? Jackpot now I've scored.

I'm dating such a pretty girl,
We went down to the beach
You want to swim, I want a whirl,
Chasing jackpot I can't reach.

Roll of the dice

I wouldn't get involved in fun,
I'm planning gambling trip
I think I am the only one,
The gambling not the dip.

I've spent all of my money,
I feel like such a pratt
I know it isn't funny,
It's time for heading back.

I cannot spend my time with you.
All I want to do is gamble
I'll lose a love so very true,
Explain but then I ramble.

I've realised I have a habit
I gamble every day
I know I'm being tragic but,
I've lost you anyway.

If I don't have the funds
To fix my selfish needs
I do it all, then I run
I know this brings on greed.

I've lost a very special one
because I'm very mean
I realise there is no more fun,
I need to sort and clean.

Roll of the dice

It's tragic when I ponder back,
The wealth that I have spent
Gambling on the booze and that,
Inhibitions got quite bent.

I tried to stop the gambling,
I tried to stop the show
But still I chase the only thing,
I won't stop so here I go.

I'm betting on the horses now
Grand national, it's quite tense
I'm wondering just why and how
Mine fell at the first fence.

When after work in local pub
I play the fruit machine
It's time for you to get your grub,
For me I chase the dream.

I've started backing football now,
A win or both to score
I use my brain on this one
How I've never tried before.

I'm getting very good at this,
I've won a princely sum
I watch the final score don't miss,
It's tense but really fun.

Roll of the dice

I know the bubbles gonna burst,
We'll meet up for a coffee
Decide on which team is the worst,
Can't seem to win for toffee.

I tried to kick the habit
And I realized I can't stop
The seasons getting very bland,
It's time to stop the rot.

I tried to go cold turkey
To stop the gambling spree
I managed maybe thirty days of
being gambling free.

But once I've had my fill of booze
I'd always crash again
I'd drink another pint but lose
The gambling was my friend.

I've worked out that I'm hopeless
Gambling, booze and fags
At one point I was useless
No defense but now I'm sad.

I will give up my old habits,
Don't want it any more
I know I am an addict
And clean life I will adore.

Time

There's something that we all possess
That makes us stand out from the rest
Don't matter whether feeling sad
There is this thing that we all have.

A precious thing, but use it well
Make a difference, but never tell
If people feel both sad and blue
Don't get upset they turned to you.

This thing it moves both day and night
It never stops whatever the plight
It's not for money which we need
To say it costs is just pure greed.

To give this shows you really care
Don't matter whether just or fare
Rich or poor or lowly man
Can give this gift, a helping hand.

Tomorrow just a day away
But why not change the world today
You see the precious thing is time
Costs nothing to see that people are fine.

Use it well, look out for friends
And make sure there's a happy end
Because one day it could be you
Who needs their time to get you through.

Time

The clock is always ticking by
As sure as stars light up the sky
But do not wish your life away
Do not regret you did not say.

If someone, stranger, friend or other
Mother, son, daughter or brother
Needs your time then don't despair
Give up your time because your there.

So if you feel you won't get through
Turn to me my friend, I'm there for you
And hope the favour is returned
If I need help for my concern.

Heavy heart must cross this road
Compassion, care and time you showed
Makes a difference to the less
And needy people have no stress.

Look forward to each and every day
And never wish your time away
Use it wisely, both heart and soul
With help at hand you'll reach your goal.

Should people feel the need to ask?
For your advice then put to task
All that you know and make it fine
And give up some of your precious time.

Ugly

Can you explain one thing to me
That when so young ignore my plea?
Too blind to notice didn't see
How this would shape my future.

Dread the night that you went out.
Have to abide or get a clout.
Don't care if cry or scream and shout.
Put up with this my torture.

Always live in fear and dread,
If it's not his at school instead.
All the names but mostly pleb
But no-one seems to care.

People always wondered why
I was so lonely, always cry.
It doesn't matter what I try
This life just isn't fare.

Do you still stand by what you meant
You told me I was an accident?
An ugly baby away was sent.
I know I was not wanted.

Ugly

Why did you all treat me so bad?
You don't know how it made me sad.
My doctor told me now I'm mad.
My head the seed was planted.

Undo the damage will take years
I don't have normal hopes and fears.
One day who knows cry happy tears
And have a normal life.

Remember when I scored the winner.
Of course you don't just wine then dinner.
I don't believe was born a sinner.
Play god the usual strife.

As a child should never be,
A favorite but you don't see.
You favored him well above me,
Again I'm afterthought.

I wasn't planned by dad and you
You never stopped to see it through.
Create a life no matter who,
Self-harm is all I sought.

Ugly

Why don't you see the man I am,
Created by the family hand.
Embarrass you I always can
Unless you see the truth.

My life screwed up not a good start.
Traumatic life you have an art.
But did you bank on my kind heart,
Forgive you for my youth.

You seem to think I do not get
How I came to be and fret.
It's not our fault but don't forget
My weird and mad behavior.

When I destruct I always know
That I am not some freak side show.
Just nurture me and let me grow.
I never found my savior.

Convenient to blame the drink
But did you ever stop to think.
Don't matter how much that I sink,
Without my pills I worsen.

Is it so wrong to blame my past?
These feelings, pain will always last.
My knowledge good and memories vast.
You created me this person.

My Journey with alcohol

I don't know if I was born this way
Or was it learnt behaviour
As I could drink all day and night
Even though I hate the flavour.

It's not the taste that floats my boat
It's not the taste I like
Just need to get that fuzzy head
To make me feel alright.

The first time that I sunk that ship
I thought drinking so much liquor
would make all of us feel grown up so
We swigged it then got sicker.

I'd started smoking way before
The first time I got plastered
I started young, before my time
If only I had mastered.

If the one's I look up to
Can make it look so cool
Then why do I keep passing out
And always play the fool.

The first time that I bought my pint
I was 15 getting ready
But straying off the narrow path
My drinking became quite needy.

My Journey with alcohol

So leaving school the hopes where high
I thought I'd go to college
With a steady mind I thought
All that's missing is the knowledge.

If I could just hold down a job
And learn and have a wage
Master the devil that is booze
But then I met you Dave.

Before that time my only vice
Was gambling and tobacco
Add alcohol to that long list
It makes thing's tough and wacko.

Thing's got very rough for me
I couldn't keep on course
I'm in the lead in life's long race
But I fell of the leading horse.

I'd like to say that at this point
I finally got a handle
Drinking became a hurricane
I started going mental.

In a drunken foggy haze
I broke the law in style
I thought they would go soft on me
But Instead I walked the mile.

A girl she made a promise true
When I get out we'd make it
Relations very toxic and
My drinking took you, Tragic.

My Journey with alcohol

It wasn't long before we split
I couldn't take the grief
It was then I booked a holiday
To sunny Tenerife.

I borrowed money from the branch
To fund my drinking habit
Boarded the plane from lie and chance
No job for me so damn it.

I came back to a single life
With no girlfriend in my way
So I will keep on drinking
And forget I cannot pay.

So the turning point they thought
Was meeting future lover
We'd have a child and others too
But again I could not cover.

Job after job, drink after drink
I got very low in mood
Even though I had it all
The family and the brood.

But once again I broke the law
The pressure took the lot
I thought that I lost everything
My freedom, kids the plot.

My Journey with alcohol

Coming home we made the move
To rural pastures new
I took a steady well paid job
But long before I knew.

My drinking and my gambling
Got completely out of sink
I figured if I just quite one
The other stuff not the drink.

So once again I'm on my own
I know you couldn't take it
Kicked into touch, I'm all alone
I've found the shoes that make it.

It probably took me many years
To finally see the problem
I have my drinking issue
And the pain is very gruesome.

The Gp said "just stop the booze"
It really sounds straight forward
I cannot find a way to stop
Even though it's getting awkward

.I always took a hostage for
The journey in my life
But now I'm sat here on my own
I'm sick of all this strife.

My Journey with alcohol

One more time I'm taken ill
I'm waiting to be seen
A gastric problem diagnosed
The penny drops right in.

I pondered what you said to me
On the way back to my flat
I find a full unopened gin
I can't be doing that.

Down the sink I pour the booze
I finally agreed
I am an alcoholic
And I feel somewhat relieved.

So I'm off to my first meeting
And I look like death warmed up
I wonder will it be released
I know I'm all washed up.

I sit here read the 12 by 12
Don't understand your logic
Your not alone I heard you say
First meeting not quite got it.

The key is very easy though
Just one day at a time
Is all it takes to pay the price
And soon you will be fine.

My sponsor helps me through the steps
I know you have my back
The other good advice I took
Was just keep coming back.

A loss of liberty

Prison is a harsh regime,
The toughest life that's ever been
Think you'll survive then think again
Heed my words I'll save you pain.

Look everywhere and find support
Was not my fault I just got caught
Why does it have to be this way?
Same old rubbish just different day?

Just look around at what you've got
In this old place you've lost the lot
Everything and liberty
Have a heart and set me free.

Everyone's a number here
A dear John is the greatest fear
Fortnightly visit the only thing
That makes sense of my daily sin

A weekly shop on canteen day
A chance to spend my meagre pay
Attend their groups for sound advice
Tobacco being my only vice

Don't matter how tough life can get
A prison life you won't forget
In here you have to tow a line
Unspoken rule of prison time.

A loss of liberty

My greatest fear when I come home
That love we shared is all but gone
So studied for my C and G
To get a job when I am free.

To carry on and live this way
Can guarantee in here you'll stay
Unless you learn you cannot win
The prison system you'll always be in.

Don't take that life you have a choice
When things go bad then use your voice
Ask for help and make a stand
If you get stuck I'll lend a hand.

Don't forget was in your shoes
Always react, a small lit fuse
But then I worked out what it means
Just like you now I have those dreams.

Never back to those dark days
No more struggle and cloudy haze
I have the strength to see it through
Paid my price, but now just like you.

That life for me has all but gone
Let's lock him up as he did wrong
I paid my price you got it all
Except this thing, my heart and soul.

A loss of liberty

Already been judged for my crimes
And served it through, I've done my time
I never meant to hurt, deceive
I'm going straight you must believe

I have my dream of being free
And live my life controlled by me
It will get tough, temptation and strife
But I will live an honest life.

The turning key the slamming door
I don't deserve that life no more
For I have served my time for you
What else is left for me to do.

The doubt you hold is will I stray?
The only thing I need today
2.4 a dog called spot
Suburban semi with a plot.

The easy thing for me before
Was how to bend and break the law
Time to pack my bag and go
And say farewell to all I know.

A handshake, say goodbye to you
So long to only life I knew
Stroll out the gate and have a try
The man left there has waved goodbye

Capel shuffle

I didn't mean to do it
I lost the plot again
I tried to reason, do my best
I'm empty feeling pain.

The hospital I'm back again
The section looming fast
I justify it every time
This is not going to be the last.

Waiting for the jolly trolley
One and two plus three
One brings your meds; two brings the food
And three a cup of tea.

Walk the Capel shuffle
Attacks of fear and panic
I cannot go no faster
As my mood is very manic.

It's hard to talk and let it out
I can't explain it sadly
Always flout and bend them all
The rules you dish out gladly.

Where is my medication
I want to go to bed
I over did things can't you tell
I have a pounding head.

Capel shuffle

What is the point in all this fuss?
I'm really not that bad
Four policemen, cuffed up, locked away
When really I'm just sad.

If only you would listen
You would see it's not that way
No doubt I'll stay in here again
No matter what I say.

When I get out it starts again
I don't know how to stop
I'll take your pills and your advice
But I know I'll lose the plot.

I'll be seeing you next month
Who knows I may just learn
That one day given right advice
A corner I may turn.

Until the day we meet again
I'll try and keep it real
You'll never understand my pain
My world you cannot feel.

If we were somewhere else I know
You'd treat me as your equal
No more from me there's no more show
I just pray there's not a sequel.

Father

Sitting on the corner.
Watch the world go by.
Think about the dad I've lost.
A tear comes to my eye.

Everyone is staring.
Wonder why I'm sad.
Why do I miss the old man so?
And all the times we had.

I do not have the answer.
Just why I miss you so
I wasn't really close to you.
Just really need to know.

I do not have a photo.
There's nothing left for me.
Nothing but a memory.
Of a world you did not see.

Saturday was our day.
When my team play at home.
A moment to forget it all.
If only you had known.

Don't want to spoil the moment.
Treasure this happy time.
For this the one and only day.
That everything is mine.

I never said exactly.
Just what I'm going through.
Thing's could have been so different.
Deep down I think you knew.

Father

We got our time together.
When your life was soon to end.
Poured out my heart and soul to you.
Too late my life to mend.

No mention at your passing.
It's like I don't exist.
The night you lost your battle.
Betrayed my feelings with one kiss.

You said you thought you lost me
But made of sterner stuff
You broke my heart when you left home
Sorry isn't good enough.

You've seen me battle illness
And face my darkest foe
I needed you to fight for me
Protect me as I grow.

But as I got much wiser
And grew from family curse
I realized it isn't all about me
Your problems where much worse.

We had a family curse for sure
Born from alcohol and temper
Those shoes they fitted nicely
For the journey but I surrender

Father

Don't want to live the secrets of
The life that we all hide
The curse I'll take it to my grave
With me the problems die.

As mentioned words from one of us
It's like a flower bed
With every generation passed
We plant more flowers instead

I wouldn't change my life again
I tried to play the game
But when I got to say goodbye
I didn't want to be the same

The battle which I'm facing
Is mine and mine alone
Depression, darkness everywhere
In defeat the way was shown.

When I get down and lonely.
Look to the star filled night.
Remember, cherish happy times
Because now you know I'll be alright.

Self harm

Laying here, the hospital bed
Thinking back on what you said
Ten hours ago I thought was dead
But now I've changed my mind.

It seems to happen now and then
The first time maybe nine or ten
But got much worse then way back when
The path I always find.

The scars I bear for my self-harm
Mostly pills or cut my arms
Does not matter it makes me calm
Another night of hell.

Just stop and think about my plight
What makes me carry on this fight?
You're never wrong, I'm never right
You all know I'm unwell.

I know it's hard to have respect
For one like me, I won't forget
It went too far, I do regret
This time it nearly cost me.

But carry on none the less
Life for all is but a test
Give me this one, forget the rest
The scars for all to see.

I've never really worked out how
The reason why I lay here now
My self-harm seems the only pal
That understands my madness.

Self harm

When I get down the pills I pop
Why do I always try to top?
People wish I would just stop
It's the only cure for sadness.

Most times I'm caught or just confess
Not easy living with the stress
When things get tough I'll fail the test
Can bank on me to stumble.

I haven't done this for a while
But still I walk the lonely mile
Chalk up another one on file
I'm all patched up and humble.

I always try to run away
But it don't matter where I stay
The devil knows to whom I pray
And tempts me every turn.

It's like a drug for which I hunger
Don't think I could have coped much longer
But wiser now I'm feeling stronger
One day I may just learn.

I know it's mad and quite insane
An overdose and cut again
Why carry on with all this pain
What made me do the deed?

Self harm

The most important thing is this
They'll never be a perfect bliss
My life there's always things amiss
It's an addiction which I need.

So will I stop? You never know
I may just put on one last show
I have the need to let it go
I will give it one last try.

If you forget all I have done
Believe me this was never fun
Support me, let me see the sun
Give me wings so I may fly.

I have to battle darkest blues
Throw in the towel is all I knew
Euphoric highs then desperate moods
Prepared to shout out loud.

There is no cure for one like me
But have some faith as you can see
The seed of youth is now a tree
I'm standing tall and proud.

Self-destructive kind of lifestyle
May get you through for a short while
But one step forward then back a mile
I'm sick of all this pain.

I can promise you this one small thing
That late at night the phone won't ring
The casualty I won't be in
Try not to do it again

The local

When growing up within a mile
We had several pubs to choose
I could make them all my local
With many friends and booze.

I'll get involved with all the games
My local has it all
Bar Billiards was my choice of game
And sometimes darts and pool.

I do a geographical
My local pub has changed
For every time that I up sticks
I find within my range.

Each town I stay I always find
My favourite drinking spot
I make myself quite comfy
As I think I've found my lot.

So what I thought was final move
To a town I know quite well
There is a pub across the street
Two minutes from where I dwell.

My local is my favourite place
The one I love the most
After work or long weekends
I'll drink to that, your toast.

I always drink here every day
But something's feeling wrong
I clock the way you look at me
And wonder what I've done.

The local

I have a job to pay my way
Would you like another drink
Today I feel left out, confused
I ponder back and think

I don't want any aggro from
The place that I get tight
But I see the way your acting
Pretty sure we'll have a fight.

It's clear you want to hurt me
I can see it in your eyes
Just one of me, for you there's three
But here is the surprise.

I always choose to walk away
I'll find somewhere else to booze
I've over stayed my welcome
If we fight I know I'll lose.

Bigger man I'll always be
I learnt to walk away
No point to prove as you can see
There's nothing more to say.

So you look tough before your mates
Well done its nothing different
Go home and when it starts to grate
Who knows I might just listen.

The local

So I will find another pub
Move on to pastures new
Anything would be better then
Sharing a drink with you.

Instead of drinking socially
I always took my fill
I over stayed my welcome
Over the road or up the hill.

So once again I'm on the move
Back to where it all began
A nice flat with a local pub
Maybe this time I'll hatch a plan.

But this drinking game is different
There's no acrid smoke no more
No closing time, saloon bar
And not dirty sticky floor.

To you I'm just some punter
With cash to burn and spend
But little did you know of me
I started this morning at ten.

There's two pubs I can choose from
The cocktails go down nice
Happy hour will get me tight
Two lagoons please and some ice.

The local

You barred me from your drinking fun
Knocked over drinks and table
I plead with you that I can change
I'm barred even though I'm able.

There's only one more drinking hole
For me to get my fix
I guess I'll drink alone at home
It's cheaper than you think.

I justified my drinking days
It was a rite of passage
But now I down a lot of booze
My drinking getting tragic.

I haven't gone to the local pub
My bodies had enough
An alcoholics way of life
Costs too much and just gets rough.

It doesn't float my boat no more
The local I don't miss
Can't justify my local pub
I've saved my life from this.

If I go back to my local
It would tempt again the devil
So if you find me sitting there
I'll drink orange and lemon soda.

Life of an alcoholic

When I wake up, get out of bed
Bleary eyed and pounding head
The kettle on and fag for me
Jeremy Kyle on ITV.

The weekend past it's Monday now
Try to resolve the latest row
Feed the cat and plan the day
Post is here, more bills to pay.

Brush my teeth and comb my hair
Look in the mirror for wear and tear
Catch the bus go into town
A small drink and a long sit down.

With headphones in and music on
Won't move an inch until I'm done
Window shop I can afford
Trying hard to not get bored.

Same people sat behind their till
To serve me quick and ready meal
Big issue not today thank you
No time to stop just passing through.

Check the phone when I come home
A cold call from complete unknown
Put kettle on, turn on the box
Check teletext for last results.

Life of an alcoholic

Washing up and mop the floor
Ignore the knock at my front door
Phone up my bro for a quick chat
Meet for a beer I could do that.

Hop on the bus, chug up the hill
Meet up with you and our friend Phil
A few beers and the world to rights
Alas my friends bid fond goodnight.

Last bus is due I must depart
Four pack at home can't wait to start
Micro meal it's time to eat
And rest the not so weary feet.

Watch the telly, same old stuff
One hundred channels not enough
Tomorrow chippy, rock and chips
Ignore his ABBA's greatest hits.

Beer in one hand the other a ciggie
Ponder my day and feel quite giddy
This seems to be the only way
to get me through another day.

Take my pills it's time for bed
Tomorrow usual pounding head
The routine that I always do
Will be enough to see me through

Angels

An angel watches over thee
And guides, protects, looks out for me
You give me strength, protecting so
I do not see, but yet I know

This much is true, your always there
If others fail you always care
White feather falls upon the ground
Your way to show you are around

Heaven sent, my soul is strong
When your with me, I do belong
I love you so, I feel such pride
To know you stand right by my side

Angels wings are strong and tough
They have to be for life is rough
But by my side you always stood
At last I think I understood

You cared for me, all that I'm worth
Looked out for me, on heavens earth
Made sure I did not come to harm
And welcomed me with open arms

So spread your wings and off you fly
And soar up high into the sky
Protecting others in your care
The love you have is quite sincere

Angels

I want to be an angel too
So I can protect just like you
Your always be there when I need love
Soaring high over, above

When I sleep alone at night
All snuggled up warm and tight
I know your there because I dream
Of better times and happy things

The bravest angel forever mine
Should I dream of darkest times
You lift me up and let me rest
Angel wings are just the best

The day I said farewell to mum
Was the day I become number one
I needed support, care and love
So you came down from up above

I feel your presence every day
I hope you never go away
If it's my time and I am done
I will never forget your number one

When my time is up I won't deny
I hope you teach me how to fly
So welcome me I stood the test
At least with you I am at rest.

Quiz night

Who knows tonight go down our local
The usual crowd it's always vocal
We do this every single week
Don't think you care just fame you seek.

Tonight a competition on
Remember last week how you shone
How did you know the answer to?
That question, well impressed with you.

Another night like those before
Not interested with final score
Unless a question that I know
Makes me look smart, I'll steal the show.

Sometimes remember obscure things
Some history and the reign of kings
I don't know much as you can see
This night is really not for me.

Not really my thing you can tell
I'm not that bright you know full well
None the less will try to think
Off to the bar another drink.

It's fair to say you know your stuff
Unlike myself I find this tough
If I sit here appear to show
That question I will have a go.

Quiz night

Just nod my head agree with you
Are you quite sure? I never knew
I can seem bright and fit in here
Back to the bar another beer.

Half way through and in third place
Just pace ourselves it's not a race
For you it's all, for me just fun
You won't be glad until it's won.

The only thing for you is win
I see it written on your grin
Somehow if triumph all you see
That people have respect for thee.

You do not have to be the best
Sometimes it's just about the rest
I scratch my head I think I know
The answer to that question so.

Give me a chance believe in me
I'm not that thick but trust can be
It's hard for you to just admit
Believe me I am not that thick.

I sometimes know the hardest stuff
You don't believe it's not enough
You do not have the knowledge for
Depeche Mode and occasional war.

Quiz night

If it's the Beatles then you shine
For me the music of the time
Is 80's pop and sometimes bikes
Or boxing champ that won the fight.

If there's a quiz we can explore
Attend the one at my old school
Good evening sir, remember me
I'll drink my beer because it's free.

I still smoke, you remember when
You caught me smoking way back when
Detentions owed when I left school
Remember that, but now I'm cool.

This quiz is tough, there's better teams
The likes of which I've never seen
We do our best but we don't win
No triumph for returning king.

You tried your best but just accept
There's only us were not the best
Final score we come in 5th
Although were bright you can't resist.

To have a pop and pass the blame
I hate it all and also name
Were so much more at usual haunt
The lesson that were always taught.

Quiz night

Is stay upon familiar patch
And ponder, think and have a scratch
Prefer to go along that night
We'll win again, I know I'm right.

I don't enjoy the night with you
You always made me feel so blue
If we don't win you lose the plot
And blame me as I have forgot.

A pattern you can see appear
Not here for quiz only for beer
I've had my fill of beer and you
Enough to last a lifetime through.

We'll chew the fat the usual spite
You never ask if I'm alright
Just win the quiz at any cost
For me don't care if we come last.

Nearly over, time to run
The final score my god we won
I must admit don't like the thrill
When I am drunk my mood you kill.

I know you are my brother and
This much I think I understand
Don't change a thing because we won
Next week just try and have some fun.

Mr Crazy

I'd like to say I live alone
But that statement isn't true
Cause every step I choose to take
I'm followed round by blue.

I went to do my shopping
But when I reached the town
I realised now I'm not alone
I'm being followed by frown.

Painkillers for my headache
To try and numb the pain
Try and reason with myself
But followed now by insane.

Get off the bus and wander
Go home to empty pad
But again I'm being followed
By the other one called mad.

I think I'll call my friend up
To have a chat, confess
But suddenly it's all too clear
I'm being stalked by stress.

I'll sit down watch a movie
Beer, fag no ifs no buts
Pretend I cannot see you
Sitting over there is nuts.

Mr Crazy

Feeling bored and tired
The housework I avoid
Answer the phone that's ringing
Have a chat with paranoid.

Run a warming bath for me
The water soft and gentle
Dry myself and brush my hair
Staring back is that bloke mental.

Sit down and have a beer, t v
Right now I feel quite lazy
Send a text to stay in touch
With old friend Mr Crazy.

Every day's a problem
For every day I'm sick
But just because I'm slightly mad
Doesn't mean to say I'm thick.

To spend a day in my shoes
To live the life I feel
You'll see I don't enjoy this life
I hate it when I'm ill.

Not lonely if I'm honest
Not always feeling pain
But always share my life with them
And tomorrow will be the same.

The boy past my window

Your clothes are somewhat tatty,
Shoes worn and full of holes
Despite the dreary weather
I see your frozen toes

Every day I see a boy
Walking down my street
Never looking straight ahead
But always at his feet

You seem to be quite troubled so,
Why do you look so glum
Where do you travel every day,
What do you do for fun

I want to call out to you
And ask you for your name
Then maybe we could get to share
Our misery and pain

The weather doesn't stop you,
I see you every day
The anguish etched upon your face,
Dare you stop and say

A little glance to show to me
You noticed I was there
But lonely forlorn desperate face,
So sad full of despair

I stare out in the pouring rain
And see you shuffling slow
Every day you stroll along
To where no-body knows

The boy past my window

Don't know if others see you,
But rest assured young man
If you need help with your burden,
I'll lend a helping hand

An hour, a day, a week, a month,
The last time that I saw
A weary saddened lonely boy,
Strolling past my door

Many days have passed by now
Before I knew just why
The reason for your absence
The day you said goodbye

If only you too could see the pain
That is etched upon my face.
I see you every single day
The slow and saddened pace.

I wish I could just take away
All of your saddened fears
But alas I cannot take away
Your sad and lonely tears

You made a vow to visit,
To sit there at her stone
To show how much you love her,
And tell her she's not alone

The loneliness got too much,
The pain you couldn't hide
To the day just one year later,
Once again your by her side

Fate

I never thought that I could be
A part of love and family
I saw you sitting over there
And wondered do I really dare.

Decide to go the long way home
Go back to only life I've known
But as I ran down the Westway
My name you called I heard you say.

I turned to see who called my name
The girl before, the very same
The one that trapped my gaze before
Is this my fate dare I ignore.

We got some food and have a chat
All pile back to your council flat
In the kitchen food to eat
Talked all night, massaged your feet.

The sun is up its time to go
Give me your number you never know
Took me the best part of three days
To find the courage to meet your gaze.

The man you married was not right
He would not sit and talk all night
Not like we did on that first time
I knew that I was yours, you mine.

We both can see this is our fate
Can't walk away and make mistake
Your ex I thought he'd never do
The desperate thing's to keep with you.

He pushed me to the brink and more
The flames and bang at our front door
It's just too late to run and hide
I love you so I must decide.

Fate

To live in fear but stay with you
No going back, our family grew
My baby girl you're here with me
Welcome to the family.

People said we'd never last
Cause we both have baggage and a past
We'll prove them wrong, we're meant to be
Another for the family.

Worked too hard to earn some pay
I'm working every single day
I'm not ignoring you, just tired
I need another job, just fired.

I didn't notice this before
But once that I am out the door
He'd come around and worm his way
The right words that he'd always say.

You don't know how you broke my heart
When you and he met in the park
Tried to pretend, forget it all
And take our older child to school.

No going back the trust has gone
But equally I'm just as wrong
Ignored your needs, I'm to blasé
Just one more chance for me to say.

You where the one, I let you go
I know it's too late for me to show
If only we could turn back time
Forgive you when you crossed that line.

To be quite honest I loved you more
Than anyone else there was before
I can forgive cause now I see
That me and you were meant to be

More than friends

Out of sight and out of mind
A chance to show to me you're kind
A pleasant dream, a happy theme
The joy of love, a happy scene.

I know so well but can you tell
A lonely solitary bell
Rings out aloud and makes me proud
One chance for me to say out loud.

A lonely place, etched on your face
But trust me you are no disgrace
Stand by my side and never hide
The stuff I know you feel inside.

Despite the fuss it's hard to trust
I never share what we discuss
Just give it time, you will be fine
Inside your heart you'll always shine.

Look to the sky and dry your eye
I never like to see you cry
If you are part then we can start
To try and mend that broken heart.

I know it's rough, life can be tough
And some days you have had enough
Please try to mend for people depend
They need you in their lives again.

People pay cause they don't say
Just what you mean to them today
A slippery slope but still you cope
But please do not give up your hope.

More than friends

For both of us we want the same
To be happy, calm and very sane
Stay with him you'll never win
I'll show you where your life begins

Let go be free the troubling life
It's in the past you're not his wife
So sad so glum, there is no fun
The past will catch you if you run

A tale to tell, you know it well
We both have our own padded cell
There is no end cause you will mend
And I will always be your friend.

So if you stay with us today
Then we can take your pain away
And maybe so you never know
The brightest star up there will show.

You can't be wrong if you stay strong
Despite you feel you don't belong
So don't feel blue, he shines for you
For your a precious angel too

A Permanent solution to a temporary problem

The end is nigh, no need to cry
Offer prayers to darkened sky
You know my soul is going to fry
Wish me all the best.

I will give in, know I can't win
My life so full of un-said sin
But don't know where it did begin
A constant searching quest.

No going back I cannot hack
The pressure in my life did stack
My heart so heavy all is black
I'm gloomy, pessimistic.

Remember me, one day you'll see
You plant a seed that makes a tree
Just nurture, feed and set me free
My fear is too realistic.

The bitter pill it's all too real
Hard to swallow my last meal
Not floating on an even keel
All washed up feeling empty.

You say you care, that is not fare
My life somehow you can compare
To all the family strife, don't dare
Opportunities a plenty.

A Permanent solution to a temporary problem

I've given up the pain won't stop
Too many drugs my blood won't clot
You'll never beat the family rot
Release me from my hell.

The prophecy for all to see
Condemn my life since age of three
Take me off the family tree
It's time to say farewell.

Blame my peers for all my fears
Rubbish hoarding this for years
I'm racing through emotion gears
How I end I will decide.

Mood is high, I cannot cry
I gaze upon the starry sky
And wonder do I want to die
Forgiveness I can find.

The end is near I have no fear
Raise your glass and give a cheer
And watch me slowly disappear
The legacy I leave.

A coward's end please don't defend
I've done it now too late to mend
For all to see I can't pretend
My life now you believe.

Faith

The sun is setting, made it through
Another day good night to you
I know that when tomorrow comes
I'll struggle through its never fun.

The door is always open for
Anyone that needs to pour
And others feel the need to pray
Let it out to him will say.

There's trouble brewing the horizon
But just sit here can be surprising
A time to ask for help with grief
I'm here each day still no belief.

Not sure I need a man of faith
To stop me being the disgrace
Opinions of the man upstairs
Would one day answer all my prayers

Not searching for that blinding light
Just want to make it through tonight
Have problems everywhere I look
Sit quietly and read your book.

I know my life is in a mess
Don't think I understand your test
Three of four times every day
I stroll up here to have my say.

Faith

I always walk the same way round
And still I search cause have not found
What made me walk this different way?
When coming up the church to pray.

I find my solace in your ways
I feel it's written for different days
It's not for me or so I thought
Is it true it can't be bought

A faith that works is personal
Get right sized and feel quite humble
So try again, just one more go
I'll keep the faith, the one I know

All my fear is leaving me
Arms outstretched I look to thee.
And there it was just one more step
Before my eyes at last I get.

I found your clue the lesson subtle
At last I feel I've won the battle
Ask it shall be given you
I did not ask but my god knew.

When in life don't feel you'll cope
Do not be sad there's always hope
If I can see it so can you
With faith at side you will get through.

Epilogue: Let it go.

I am a new man these days and I hope a better father, but the truth is I could have been a statistic.
That was me, my life, my hell and my journey.
I could have jumped off at any time but I couldn't.
The thought of getting sober scared the hell out of me.
Despite having two wonderful daughters
whom I adore I couldn't stop drinking.
I have other issues too which was written in the book also.
My journey with alcohol started from a very young age.
I couldn't just have one, it had to be oblivion.
I did some crazy stuff and yes I was drunk at the time.
You see I was always drunk, well unless I was in prison or hospital. I have siblings and they turned out alright.
I am not saying, "it's not fair, poor me", if you had my life,
and so on. I was just different.
I had to concede that my mental health was caused by my childhood and is what it is. I have a diagnosis and I am on medication and that side of my life is under control.
As long as I keep taking my medication I am reasonably alright.
The gambling was another issue I had to deal with.
If you combine undiagnosed mental health issues, gambling and alcoholism what could possibly go wrong?
My rock bottom and my life took a turn on the 18th June 23.
I was close to losing not only my council flat but my entire life.
I was scared, this was it, on the streets or dead.

I ended up in casualty with a gastric problem. The IT system had crashed and I was a smoker at that time.
I got talking with a lovely woman called Sharon that night
and her husband bought me a cup of tea. She was so kind and we talked all night. She gave me a cuddle when
I was getting into my taxi and she said "you can do this".
I can do what? You can stop drinking I can see it in your eyes.
I pondered this on the journey home which seemed to take forever.
In the fridge was a new bottle of rum so I cracked it open.
I wasn't going to drink this one, this one was for the drain.
I called AA and that night I went to my first meeting.
Scared? Hell yes but I had reached my rock bottom.
Many people in the past had told me I was an alcoholic, but I would always deny it but finally the penny dropped.
Just like that, a kind stranger that gave me her time, that was all
I needed. I have never seen Sharon again but she is my angel.
I have other angels too, my daughters are on the top of that list
as is their mother. I hadn't talked with them for 9 years but after a good few months of sobriety I reached out.
I can happily say I have them in my life again
and I even quit smoking.
The point is no matter how bad your life
seems there is always a chance if you have the capacity to be honest.

Acknowledgements

My list to all the people that have helped me is vast. My life could have been so different had I not got sober. People say you get a life beyond your wildest dreams but I thought that was just a saying. The truth is you do get a life beyond your wildest dreams if you work the program. I was always struggling with issues, some I blame myself and selfishly I blame others. Its easier to blame other people for the way I became. I struggled from my earliest memories, always blaming my parents. However, my late mother, despite all her faults did a pretty remarkable job. She raised 4 children on her own, whilst working 3 jobs just to provide for us. My regret is that she never saw me get sober. In my family the male gene should come with a health warning. I would like to thank my brother Larry who shared some words of wisdom with me. As my family goes the history of the men was very predictable. Generation after generation had issues, drinking, fighting, prison, the list is endless. Larry explained to me that our family is like a garden, its full of weeds. However, with each new generation we pull up more weeds and plant more flowers. I totally related to this analogy.

The support and love from my daughters has been epic. Both Charlotte and Megan came to a meeting to see me receive my 2 year sobriety chip. It blew my mind, something which seemed impossible when I started my journey. They tell me all the time how proud they are of me and I have the best job on the planet, to be their Dad. I used to hate June. My belly button birthday and fathers day. It is the same month I have my sobriety birthday now. I get to celebrate all 3 as I get spoilt by both my girls. We spend a lot of time together now and talk every day. Charlotte suffered from a brain tumor and at the time our worlds came crashing down. I was in charge of fetching and carrying and doing school runs. Yvonne, her mum stayed with Charlotte in hospital and showed immense strength and courage, something she has always had.

The start of my journey begins from a chance encounter. I was in hospital having treatment for a gastric problem. I got talking to a lovely woman called Sharon. I was in casualty for 7 hours and myself and Sharon got talking. She was so kind to me and her husband bought me a cup of tea. I never got her last name but I will never forget her. When she said "you can do this", something switched on in my brain. For years people have been telling me I must or I have to but not one person said you can. For the first time in my life I was in control. I was a mess, a huge mess but she sowed that seed in my brain. With her words of wisdom I went home, pondering what had just happened. It hit me, in a subtle and calm way I had hit my rock bottom.

Another person I would like to thank is a social worker called Margaret Billinge. She believed in me when others didn't. I had the wrong diagnosis and no place to live. She completely changed my life and I will never forget her. She got me somewhere to live with Transform housing who I would like to acknowledge too. I shared a house with 2 other people who became good friends over time. When it was time to move to my own flat with Transform I met a neighbour Ian. He became a good friend and encouraged me to pursue my passion for playing music.

Writing poetry for me was just a way of expressing myself and telling a story. If I wasn't encouraged by Charlotte my poems would still be in a shoebox gathering dust. I am a very humble man today and very grateful for every day. A life beyond your wildest dreams? Perhaps so but I know one thing I am very happy today and if that is a life beyond your wildest dreams then that will do me.

To my daughters

www.ingramcontent.com/pod-product-compliance
Lightning Source LLC
Chambersburg PA
CBHW041926090426
42743CB00020B/3455